Please return/renew this item by the last date shown on this label, or on your self-service receipt.

To renew this item, visit **www.librarieswest.org.uk** or contact your library

Your borrower number and PIN are required.

Libraries**West**

AVALANCHE BOOKS

Published in Great Britain by Avalanche Books, England 2018

Printed by SRP, England

The moral rights of the authors have been asserted.

British Library Cataloguing in Publication Data. A catalogue record for this book is available from the British Library.

ISBN: 978 1 874392 02 6

Supported using public funding by
ARTS COUNCIL
ENGLAND

LOTTERY FUNDED

Contents

Winter

Spring

Summer

Autumn

FOREWORD

From time immemorial, the four seasons of the year have commanded a creative response from awed, mystified and fascinated poets and artists,

    This collection upon the theme, harvests an enduring enchantment and draws together a compelling range of magnificent contemporary poetry and prose. All the works meticulously chosen for their masterful ability to evoke the character and emotion of the changing seasons. Containing a panoply of colour, it is a resplendent and dramatic selection of new and previously published pieces which not only portray the endless wonder and beauty of nature itself, but which often forges further into a poignant commentary on life and human nature. From the whimsical and light-hearted to the profoundly emotional, all of these pieces offer us a sense of enlightenment and belonging. A flavour of how it feels to live, to love, and to be nourished so completely by the natural world.

Deborah Gaye, editor

Winter

MURMURATION

How did each one know how to glide
– forward or back or to whichever side
across the sky this January dusk?

On second guessing wings
They swerved and turned in time
fluid, as one – they moved in rhyme

so synchronised it seemed absurd.
Who'd guess, at dark
that we could be as birds?

Kathryn Daszkiewicz

THE GREEN PLOVER (LAPWING)

I see you stand in the cold mud where all
your crest and glossy colours
smudge and dull

beside the loud insistence of the gulls
by which you wait subdued
and rather small.

Emperor of fields, this is your winter life
where mud will feed you, melt the snow and hail.
Birds do not live for pride. Pulse must not fail.
The hills are stone. They whet wind to a knife.

And if this meets the mutters I have heard
from friends who moved near children by the sea
of shops, of lifts, of quiet necessity
you do not say. You wade through mud, a bird.

Alison Brackenbury

THE ICE RINK

Like skaters tracing figures on the ice,
figures of eight, circles that overlap
since no man steps in the same river twice,
on foot, by bus, we trace a mental map

of the places we pass so little changed
through all these years and of the men they link,
lovers, husbands, boyfriends, lost or estranged,
they conjure up like faces round a rink.

We are the widows, spinsters, divorcées
going round and round on our loops and pivots,
scribbling on ice melting under our blades.

They are the phantoms, daemons, devotees
who frequent our haunts, tutelary spirits,
Plato wrote, who conduct our souls to Hades.

Mimi Khalvati

WINTER SCENE

'It is an honour to be here, the great esteemed leader,'
Tom, in a letter home from Pyongyang 2016

The words you wear are heavy –
you write of water shortage – the bitter cold,

and how you've moved, enticed by a generator.
These uncensored facts can be read elsewhere.

It is cold here too, snow-flakes this morning
and your step-father wonders how you are

as he dreamt of the unimaginable
that is now your country.

He looks through the window and remembers
the excitement of the first sledge he made

and how you cried when he made you leave the park.
Night falling. All of this carried within.

Winter makes your absence stranger.
While I sleep you are closer than during the day.

In daylight I dare not think of you,
Ice on windows, frost over a lawn. These are enough.

Wendy French

SEASONS OF WINTER

These cold days are the
cost of summer, with
the crest of death stamped on

every kiss of waning sunlight.
Swallows repair to the hallowed
hush of our rueful wondering, beyond

the wing of a crimson sky, wet
with the showering drip of
inconceivable sadness.

Chris Tutton

THE DAY WE STOPPED TALKING

It was the day of 'the big snow'. The day the pipes froze
and the buses stopped. The day we couldn't see where
dogs had pissed and robins had hopped and the town
turned down its volume. No could tell who was running
away. The snow sorted that out. Cars became mute.
Heels and wheels were softened and we stopped talking.
It wasn't a decision we'd both made, it just happened for
us at the same time. There was no argument. Our silence
came sugared with grace. We'd said enough. We put our
tongues to bed and let our hands free.

That first morning our hands danced at the kitchen table
as they poured coffee or buttered toast. The cat went
cross-eyed as it watched our fingers flickering and
nipping and stroking the air. I told you how I felt so well
without opening my mouth. Our eyes, our eye brows, our
lips became important. I had never talked so much. I had
never talked so freely. There were no gaps in our
conversation. We filled our pauses with butterflies. Our
fists became buds exploding in to blossom. My hands
were no longer cold, they sang. My knuckles lost their
bluish tinge. My blood had never felt this good.

Gaia Holmes

WINTER LOVING

"Let us have winter loving that the heart
May be in peace and ready to partake
Of the slow pleasure spring would wish to hurry"
                                   Elizabeth Jennings *Winter Love*

She lies awake listening to the storm.
It breaks in through open transom lights;
runs riot through the house, a vandal gouging
pristine walls. Bringing the outside in.

She hears the garden's talk, thin as thorns
scratching glass, alpines clinging for dear life,
plastic chairs sitting themselves down hard.
And you lie close. Boats in safe harbour.

She tries to listen better, strains to hear
the scrape of firs digging in their heels
against the gale, but you snore too loudly,
content with life just lapping at your sides.

Thugs of rain shout and batter at the window
as though they'd come to sort you out. Listen!
Listen to the whale-song of the trees as they
wallow in it. See how they shake their fists.

Anne Stewart

17

LUNNA NESS

Rags and tatters of land
Pegged out in the wind;

Black, wiry grass;
Twisted hills – the distance

Veiled in rain, blind
Fold on fold – end

Where bare walls stand
And face the waves, and stare.

The sea, and nothing beyond it.
The empty shore. Behind it,

The houses without roofs.
The prayers without answer.

Katrina Porteous

WINTER WEATHERS

because Thor has been at work again
and no one ever answers the telephone
and because the persistent tone of the ring

takes me down the line to where you might be
near the upturned umbrella abandoned
on Pendine Sands or blown to sea

and because you lost umbrella after umbrella
like that blaming the new winds
the in-coming tide always finding an excuse –

because of all these things or omens of wet sands
ferocious clouds salt water seeping through shoes
and tufts of grass on the cliffs daring to raise their heads

before morning and because when you opened the door
that final time and said, *This is it* and it was it
I have to believe you're riding the amber storm

sailing the over-turned seas in a time I didn't know
and maybe you're still dancing and maybe
somewhere is that scarlet dress

Wendy French

SOMETHING IN THE HINT OF LIGHT

I'm awake and up at a run for the camera,
then waiting for the sky –
to be generous, to shift into place,
to compose itself.

And, this winter dawn, the sky is
shockingly generous…

And I capture an army of cloud, each man of it more
crimson-tinged, every serry layered in gold,

the whole battleground rolling low,
so low,

you'd feel the weight of it
would pull you down,

but for a prima dona sun, a venturesome honey ant
spreading its feelers round.

Not a moment alike as it travels the hour, rises from
                                                darkness
through every colour to Heavens Gate

only to turn robber, to settle into a grubby wash
of 50's floor-cloth grey.

And its mood turns dark – dark as an orphan planet
adrift in the Milky Way.

A generous world turned mean. The gift withheld.
The lover turned away.

If only every magnanimous dawn
could inform the whole of its day.

Anne Stewart

PRECIOUS

Tonight
up here on our
savage little island
the ice works its dark magic,
gliding and glazing
the grid of dull roads,
laminating grass
and slug tracks,
making rotten gateposts
precious,
lacquering the slipway
and turning
the harbour rocks
into hefty jewels
that we wear
around our necks
to charm
our raw-faced,
wind-flayed husbands
who know
nothing at all
about shine.

Gaia Holmes

WINTER COMES

Yesterday's smell was bare feet
on ouch-hot sand, and tomorrow
will smell of the forest road
carrying us to a lake, smooth
as leather, waxed and buffed

but today smells of old shoes found
at the back of a cupboard then chucked out
to moulder in rain and frost on a compost heap
with potato peelings, rotten tomatoes
and dottles from Grandpa's tobacco pipe;

and it's the smell of a coming storm,
of a saffron moonbeam picking out
the last moth flying alone in crazy loops
round a naked plane tree before plunging
into a story told by bitter winds.

This is the smell, not of homecoming,
but of expulsion, of tired feet searching
for the way back to summer's plateau.

Kaye Lee

THE MISTLETOE SHOW

Always hung up last thing
as if to kiss were the most daring,
the most not quite
proper behaviour on that sacred night.

It had to be full on the lips,
not just family fellowship's
chaste peck but a passionate
reminder which had been worth the wait.

She would watch him shyly
while he tied the knot, occasionally
glancing at their children then away
as if such love-play

needed innocent witnesses
to what was hardly less
than all that either could do
to hide it, a hullabaloo

of eagerness, restraint
and expectation, both of them intent
on what must follow, the tense
theatrical balance

of his stepping down, how he'd stand
beside the chair, one hand
to steady him, the other
reaching out to her

until with a sudden
rush of seasonal abandon
so exactly matching his
she would seal their Christmas kiss.

John Mole

BOXING DAY 12.45

There's something about the sky today,
as if it can't contain itself and is pink with the effort
of trying. It is pricked into submission by trees
who, anorexic ballet dancers, demand
a dramatic backdrop to their bleak contortions.

The sun smoulders whitely, its power muted
while the yellow-green back of the woodpecker
is oddly exotic among bare trunks, his hammering
amplified without summer's upholstery.

And the church, locked, hugs the secrets of its murals
as if this is the only day of the year when, like a macabre
toy shop, the damned and their tormentors wake
from mediaeval sleep to resume that grim drama
and should you put an ear to the door you'd hear
how sinners suffer for indulging.

As we climb higher, we see the city in the distance
beneath a layer of smog. And down to the south,
in whatever direction, bound to some shopping mall
with muzak and rude lighting, the M23, all fumes
and fury, is ferrying cars to the sales.

Kathryn Daszkiewicz

THE WEATHER

You're not used to this:
warmth on a dial,
double glazing,
this airless locked-in
sucked-in
almost-silence
punctuated
by the hum and tick
and bleep
of monitors, machinery
and the sticky
hush and kiss
of the nurses shoes
in the corridor
outside your tepid room.

In here
nothing flutters.
Your unread papers sleep
still and deep
whilst December
mimes a storm
outside your window

and I want to bring
the weather in.
I want to let the wind

run around you
like a rabid dog.

I want the wild rain
to lash
your thin fevered limbs
and shock you
into living.

Gaia Holmes

INSECT

Walking by the council houses in the falling snow, I thought I saw someone waving at me from a downstairs window. Yet when I got close enough to press my face against the frosty glass, I realised I had been mistaken; there was only a family watching television. Looking more closely still however, I saw myself walking on the screen. The youngest daughter was crying because the way I dragged my crushed leg behind me reminded her of an insect.

Ian Seed

THE STOVE

...And kisses on the rowan tree
The scarlet ulcers of the unseen Christ.
                          Sergei Esenin, 'Autumn'
(translated by Geoffrey Thurley)

In the big round stove they're burning up the trees.
It's hot all day in the tall kitchen. Outside
It's freezing, it's sunless as if a shadow was cast
By the ghosts of the trees that are burning, and the stove
Stays glowing all day, even when nobody's by.
They are burning the trees. All over mother Russia
The forests burn. Her face
Is darkened with smoke and labour, is grimed with soot.

They are not big trees but thin sticks of birch they're
                                              burning,
The graceful wings of pine and spruce, the blood-berried
                                              rowan.

Michael Schmidt

THE SCRIVENER

You made me a quill pen
and we dipped it in ink,

you showed me how to
scratch out words

with its yellowing
fingernail nib.

There might have been
a signature, a flourish,

yours perhaps, or mine
I should have kept,

somewhere among my things.
Now you perch

on the balcony, smoking
in all weathers, your cap

in winter, two jackets,
a scarf and gloves,

waiting for the visit
of the scrivener

31

whose hunched back
and grey wing

extend the branch below;
watching the tide,

as if, in fog or November
rain, as that grey

smoke meets the January wind,
in-between distorted cries,

those strained loudspeaker calls
of trainers to their rowing crews,

in a language that was always yours,
you hear the river sing.

Isabel Bermudez

DECEMBER

A shuffle through leaves
In childhood, whispering
Around our ankles, cross-hatch
Branches, a sickle moon.

Light with its agitation
Splintering ice,
A restless winter music
Dancing on thin air.

Welcome to our ghosts
As they come out of hiding
To warm their hands
At the fire we have made.

John Mole

FOULA, AULD YULE

6th January

Shut the door and pass the bottle
Round the circle of light.
One by one let us drink to the days
The sun makes ripe,

And join in your riddle, Aggie Jean, in the ring
Of the stove's peat reek,
While, long past midnight, the child in my lap is falling
Into sleep;

Into widening circles of sleep, that will carry her
Who knows where.
Let us drink to the fire within. We know too well
The dark out there.

Katrina Porteous

CHRISTMAS MOON

Trees hold the season's magic.
Yards of ivy skein off the bark,
red drips from holly's dark sides.

A fragment of wood
fits the child's hand like a sword.
He charges at puddles
and cuts his reflection to pieces.
The water heals over,
makes one again.

Mother wheels son home
with prickly garland.
He shouts "Hello Moon!"
"Hello Moon! Yellow Moon!"
The village is quiet, apart from him
and his friend in the sky.

Susan Taylor

APPLE TREE

Wassail night has passed and winter's
blue flames have retreated for now.
In the orchard, a thrush stabs the last
soft apple, and another calls from the tallest
tree. If you were to come by here, come
and stand by me here, I would hold
your palm to the trunk, tell you how to open
the eyes and ears of your hand so you
could feel how again the xylem and phloem
are waking, making their long slow
streaming journey between earth and star,
if you were to come here, to come by here again.

Roselle Angwin

Spring

SPRING COMES WHEN

The lark calls louder than the crow,
the brown hedge sparrow rears and sings.
Two peacock butterflies, who drowned
in plum tree flowers, weave evening's grass
dead drunk, in charge of wings.

Alison Brackenbury

PRUNING THE MAGNOLIA

The magnolia is spreading its arms
across the whole garden, juggling pink
goblets, reaching up to the roof.
It was supposed to be decorous,

a Chinese lady by the lake in pink
slippers. But it has loosed itself
from its moorings, taken ship
with a cargo of blooms, broad-leaved

and brash, colonising the delphiniums
and roses, snuffing out the red-hot pokers,
threatening to take over the garden

with a riotous party. So it has to be
pruned, clipped, curtailed,
trimmed like a poodle with a lavish pink bow.

John Daniel

THE CUCKOO AND THE EGG

After Ted Hughes' 'Amulet'

Inside the cuckoo's call, the ear of Spring.
Inside the ear of Spring, the swaying reeds.
Inside the swaying reeds, the warbler's nest.
Inside the warbler's nest, the cuckoo's egg.
Inside the cuckoo's egg, the eye of gold.
Inside the eye of gold, the tug of the sun.
Inside the tug of the sun, the bird's wings.
Inside the bird's wings, five thousand miles.
Inside five thousand miles, a vast Sahara.
Inside the vast Sahara, the overwintering.
Inside the overwintering, the hunger for young.
Inside the hunger for young, the earth greening.
Inside the earth greening, the heart's sap.
Inside the heart's sap, the cuckoo calling.

Linda France

IN THE GREEN DARK

The bindweed has snaked up (by night
it seems) under the cover of virginia creeper

charmed by the scent of honeysuckle
claiming its lovers from below, behind

in a rhythm of loops round any stalk or stem
that stops its path, pulling each partner close.

I free the poppy and the hollyhock
from this forced waltz, from the green dark

of its leaves, its crowding leaves
heart over shady heart.

Although I try (not
hard enough in spring)

to uproot each last piece
(deep from the bed)

most years it trumpets
victory from the hedge.

Maybe I'm drawn
to the darkest hearts
like a hawk moth

maybe I want
to see its white blooms fluting
the whole fence
mirroring moonlight
through long summer nights.

If only I could dare
to let it
flower.

Kathryn Daszkiewicz

SAY IT WITH FLOWERS
- a time-lapse love story

From his garden he could see her garden, as she his, from hers. He realized she was the woman from the garden centre. She'd smiled at him. He'd smiled back. He saw her hastily putting down Pride & Prejudice when he came to buy his things. She'd blushed.

He went back three days running, bought things he needed in small batches, then things he didn't need in smaller batches. "Thank you".

He earned 500 loyalty points, and they gave him a string bag of bulbs. Which gave him an idea.

He chose a patch and planted them. 'YOUR BEAUTIFUL'. No apostrophe. No e. They didn't all come up.

YO BE IF

He wondered if she'd got the message . Or any message. Probably not. Time passed.

Come Spring, after the first snowdrops, there, in neat crocuses: 'PARDON?'

Surging with adrenalin he bought two bags of bulbs. All the same this time. Fritillaries. Tenderly reiterated: 'U R

44

BEAUTIFUL'.

There, he'd said it. The wait was difficult. Then they
didn't really synchronise. While some were still just
peeking through the soil the keen ones spelt UTIFU.
The rest would catch up soon. Before they did though,
strong winds in the night flattened the UTI.
She woke to the message: FU

He panicked. He should have fluffed up the others,
propped them with sticks if necessary, instead he mowed
them all down, hoped she'd not seen.

Puzzled, but enjoying the botanical banter, she planted
blue, yellow and red primula. FU 2.

He was crestfallen. Would not trust fritillaries ever again.
Painstakingly he planted penitent red lupins. OOPS
SORRY. Then across his former lawn with cornflowers,
NO OFFENCE MEANT

Feeling for him, she replied in January, NONE TAKEN -
in snowdrops planted compassionately but perhaps not
as carefully as before. What he saw was I M TAKEN

A bitter blow. He knew what he had to do. Bravely he
planted hardy pansies, let his house and rented a flat.

She was sorry to see him go, and surprised to read
GOODBYE, GOOD LUCK.

Two years later he moved back. She spotted him, out tidying the garden the tenant had let slide.

Shyly she planted grape hyacinth. HI. He responded cautiously, in delphiniums, HI. She, in careful crocuses: R U OK?

He'd had enough. Speak and be damned. He blurted out, in unequivocal red tulips bought full-grown.'I [HEART] U'

She replied almost immediately, a smiley face in happy marigolds.

Marigolds. Marry-golds. Yes. He began to dig, his trench so deep she could read 'WILL YOU...' She went indoors to sow seeds in a tray.

Before his bulbs came up she was knocking on his door, tea-tray in hands, her eyes inviting him to pull back the covering tea-towel. Revealed, in stenciled cress, the word YES.

Matt Harvey

MARCH 4TH

I heave back the bathroom window.
The catch is stiff and, like me, old.
I would like to let in the crescent moon.
She is so slender, and must be cold.

Alison Brackenbury

SPRING CAMPING

We headed west to Wales
this year to celebrate
a special birthday, stunned
by the sheer intensity of April
blazing in wild daffodil, in celandine
and buttercup, in countless sharp stars
piercing midnight's infinity;
and in the bone-numbing cold
of pre-dawn darkness

Alwyn Marriage

YES, MY DREAM WAS REALLY SOMETHING

she tells me in her e-mail from Bucharest.
'It was Ireland. Spring. There were castles on green hills
and you drove us across a serpentine river so wide
that at first we couldn't see the other side, and the sky
bluer than cornflower, not a cloud.

At times you would slow and we'd snap images
in our minds – vivid, indelible, of reeds, bridges,
distant villages, head-high daffodils – and should we lay
our versions side by side there would be no difference,
we were so at one.' *So at one,*

the river whispers, compressing two hours of sunlight
and more than a thousand miles into the space
between two touching fingertips.

Anne Stewart

WILD GARLIC

through the sandstone bridge, she said
flows the river Spey;
where the wild garlic grows
won't you come and play?

let's play tickle trout, she sighed
whispering like the river
I would said I, *but... can't be late*
back home for me dinner

yet homewards over the mossy wall
beneath the weeping beech
Why not stay and rest awhile
her blue eyes did beseech

her blue eyes did beseech, and she
handed me some fruit,
a granny smith that began to blush
at all her talk of juice

all her talk of juice was like
a philtre drunk at bed,
it made me dream a freckled trout
was standing there instead

a freckled trout standing there,
androgynous, divine,
singing of the liquid bliss
together we would find

together we would find, she sang
fluttering her gills,
the love that breathes in silver streams,
a love for which you'd kill

a love for which you'd kill – I mused
it filled me full of doubt,
sang beneath the weeping beech
by a brown and freckled trout

a brown and freckled trout, she was
in a sequin dress
that shimmered round her swinging hips
in whisperings of bliss

whisperings of bliss that told
how – on the other side
things are more than they seem
girl   river   trout

Mark Gwynne Jones

51

LIGHT

One spring dawn, I heard someone outside singing the most beautiful song I had ever heard in a language which sounded as if it came from another time. I got up and pulled back the curtains. Through the window, I could see a youth walking across the dewy field at the back of our house. Although I was afraid, I couldn't resist waving. With a gesture he invited me to come out and join him, and I knew he would not mock me if I sang along with him, although I had no idea what it was I was meant to sing.

Ian Seed

VENUS FLOWER BASKET

Each spring,
bees appear in the grass.
The warm wakes them and
the clockwork queens tick up and set off.
They dodge my ankles
in the dash to find a nest to fatten
with family.

Gulping pollen, gulping earth,
she pulls the wax into eggs,
into the gumming clack of grubs
fed endlessly,
to grow work,
to grow an army in the thin air.

A warm noise thickens the nest
and lungs thick with sugar,
nectar-heavy, a cramp of drones and daughters
fresh from the foxgloves, thistles, knapweeds,
picnics where they licked the stick from spoons.

The nest, rattling. Frantic.
Fur bristling. Feet working.
High summer, and then,
just as quickly,
hibernation.

And the long swell of silence
surviving the winter.
The queen bled out,
a crisped shell in the chill
impossibly poised on a still wing
on the floor of the hive.

Some days I cannot think to live like that.
Some days I would rather fold up underwater,
boom to the bottom of the ocean
to crawl with the ant-sand and
pricklecrabs of tiny lights and spikes
and eyeless.

My fierce gods, my sting paling -
the whales washing overhead.
A numb noise humming.
I'd find you there –
sponge-stems like a wedding gift,
bright as silver fork-tines.
We will climb them, slip in, and stay.

We will unevolve our eyesight.
We will find new ways to learn old things
and to love old things endlessly.

And the scream of bees, and
the dull of old age – the tick of a husk
on the hivefloor –

cannot pierce the peace of blue light
and blindness.

Phoebe Nicholson

QUESTIONS

In some minds, questions never raise their heads
like crocuses that line a path in spring.
But mind has mountains, yes, and fountainheads,
streamflows that answer needs for watering.

Bring me the snowmelt then, now spring is here,
a hut on the road and my lost ancestral story,
washed clean as it is, for the wind to spear
and straggle on some hermit's morning glory.

Never ask where home is, how far away
is far away, how long ago long is.
Leave the gate open. Spiders are at home

and someone's left a straw hat, a lice comb –
an old poet who stopped here on his journey.
Borrow them, he won't mind. They're not his.

Mimi Khalvati

COW PARSLEY

Sunlight makes a home here, turns these tall stalks
        to a May haze. Intricate,
            after dull warty dock, white foam

appearing year on year
        like half-remembered lines in sleep.
Gnats, furious after the mild winter

swarm above its whiteness,
        brush my face and hair
hoverflies settle on upturned parasols of flower-heads

- dipping, quivering details.
        And I'm alive to its white noise, a cloud

which barely stirs in river-breeze,
        a lightness that won't be cut or kept in vases
swathing each side of the towpath on the Thames.

I want to run a hand through it, this thickened air.
        Grasp what it is that makes of love
a weed so ordinary and rare.

Isabel Bermudez

MADONNA OF THE PINES

No one knows how long they're alone
in the forest. Days become lampblack. Time
disappears between dim receding pillars.
Then there are needles, then needles
under needles, then soil and buried larvae.
Then she emerges from the gilt background
of the thirteenth century for Easter,
the way a fob watch sinks in a glacial lake.
A merchant found her, took her to market
and sold her. She was cleaned and unveiled.
The small spa celebrated but the bishop
wouldn't look at her. Take her down, he said.
I know who she is. I know the tricks
the pines play. She'll return your gaze
like the moon on Midsummer's Eve.
The hourglass was upended and upended
again. She threaded and unthreaded a needle
in three-quarter profile, taking care to wait
for angels like moths or for the heavens to open.
The dimple you see is mark of her patience.
Later in a private salon, after the siege,
she's robed in a blue mantle, behind her
a Tuscan hill town. It's dusk. A merchant ship
slips into harbour. It's been a hot day.
Her hands are cradling an invisible fig.
There is a verse, perhaps from a folk song,
etched on the back of a Rococo frame:
> *Mary of the green woods*
>   *Sew your soul to mine*

Smoke from the fire is drifting west
and I have red wine
Through obscure means she found herself
in Sussex, a glade, her limbs twisted
with ivy, her lips a Siddaline pout. The detail
of the flowers and her copper hair indicate
Winchelsea, October, distinguished clients.
For the twentieth century she climbed
into a box, a geometrical design extruded
into a dark dimension, a cold white crystal
beyond space and colour that started to hum
discreetly, a simple tune but old, as old
as anyone can remember.

Andrew Nightingale

VILLAJOYOSA

So that a fisherman far out at sea
returning home as the sun sank or rose,
battling fog and poor visibility
could see, rowing towards Villajoyosa,

among the seafront houses on the shore,
his own abode and by it steer his course,
each house was painted a distinctive colour:
green, ochre, terracotta, pale blue, turquoise.

Of all the blossoms that are out in May,
the lilac – Persian lilac – shares the same
lodestar quality. Never to belong

back in the wild again but to a doorway
where a stranger might hear 'death's outlet song',
it holds the past, only the past in the door frame.

Mimi Khalvati

MOTHERING SUNDAY

I heard the high raw crying of the geese.
I could not see them, which I did not mind.
But smaller in the small yard, I stood sad
that, for the first time, I was left behind.

Alison Brackenbury

MILKTHISTLE
(for my mother)

Now that I am older,
I am learning all the time from her.
In my new flat, my mother plants the pots
with certain hands
forking soil.
She blows her hair from her mouth
to tell about bolting,
blind seeds, greenfly.
She shifts and sifts handfuls,
fingers singed from courgette bristles.

From the windowsill, she whisks the crisp bodies
of wasps which had seemed before
so heavy and so poisonous.
The saplings are warm as if
slipped from her pockets.
She drops a clutch into the dirt.

I am ashamed of my long-kept, bitten plants,
of the chapped soil of supermarket herbs.
They are ungrown and shrunken –
angry and quiet as I had been all winter –
until she broke off a piece of earth
and handed it to me.

The roots slither back again and
I am small and white-fingered at our first house.

I tamper with Lambs' Ears and Milkthistle,
rubbing sap into the silt with
the compost lurking,
breathing at the bottom of the garden.
My mother, chasing aphids with soapwater,
slides fruit from the branches
like a magic trick.

She sifts these tricks into the soil now
at my new flat.
She warms and beds the tulip bulbs.

But I fear when she has gone
the flies will know I am no match and
seep back in.
I will remember her soapwater rinsing
and I will copy her fluent movement,
mimic the magic trick – and
it might work

until one day – I know –when she will
fill with soil.
Then, I will crawl inside like a blind seed
and sleep
while above
the tulips break for spring.

Phoebe Nicholson

THE STREET

So wide awake is spring now, eyes so open,
even the carpets long to fly outdoors
and prostrate themselves, carpeting the garden.
But it is only sun – bright visitors

from skylights, there at the top of the stairs,
poised to run down, brass stair rods at their heels;
is it only this sunless room which bears
a weight of shade so sculptural it feels

like Rachel Whiteread's *House* pumped full of concrete;
is it not the sensation Jorie Graham
had 'how full void is', but of void itself,

only the membrane since it has no self,
the sweet tremble of void that makes the street
cast the prefatory glow of a poem?

Mimi Khalvati

RÉPRISE

There on the wires the birds returned
Out of the south observe the town.

They look in at your window and see there
Me lying naked in your arms,

Your mouth ajar. It's not a yawn
Or snoring, it is that deep sleep

That leaves you vulnerable to dream.
I kiss your lower lip and tongue,

I touch your chin and throat, the pit
There, and the hard bone of your chest.

The birds observe us from the wire
And pass their comments back and forth.

They hang like notes on staves. I read,
More than reprise, a second theme.

Michael Schmidt

THE S WORD

The cups and frills of tête-à-tétes
at my door only make me want
more. Deeper. Longer. Your eyes
full of looking. That sweetness
in the light piques my appetite;
a lick of salt, sap knocked back
in a shot glass. Didn't we both clock
the pussy willow at the same time?

I wrap your scent around me
like a shawl, walk out into the stretch
of a lost afternoon, to the tune
of iPod-shuffled finches, Larkin's
stutter. Your F-sharp charm, here
and away, the wink of an eye.

Linda France

WANTON

Listening to the folderol of trees,
I see how buds grab at the light
and tips of wing-shaped leaves
beat at the clouds to give them flight.

Their eyes are rooted, messengers all
flying up and out as far as blue goes.
Parent branches draw from a well
where crystals drip like nascent stars.

The screen they reach for
is a covering of leaf, each moment
has a green fountain hidden in its core –
a being of the substance of abandonment.

I mark the flighty smell of pollen,
as the womb of greenwood opens.

Susan Taylor

PLANT CLEARANCE SALE

These plants are called by name:
Verbena, Petunia, Heartsease,
Geranium, Marigold, Black-Eyed Susan,
in trays and pots in shelving aisles
across a car park, where old annuals
have a last chance to sell.

Even with this year's sun and rain,
the daily metronome of English weather,
they're past their best, a few pleading petals
like dogs' eyes at a rescue kennel.
Prices on their labels show as bright
as their over-ripe blooms.

Between the racks, a tiny orb,
fairy hedgehog of a seed, stays suspended,
floats slowly just ahead as we pick plants,
like an entire dandelion head on the air.
Thistle down, hardly rare,
but free.

Simon Williams

SPRING

Winter light, northern light, catches the ridge.
    Old as stone, or the Roman Road. Dandelions,

lions-tooth, *pis-en-lit*, scatter in a fallow field

above the Pilgrim's Way. Here's the barn where a dog

    ran out and chased your bicycle. Converted; a house
                                now.
You, stealing out at night, to watch shy badgers in their
                                   setts.

Hoarding it all, for later. Now later's here. It's you and
                                  me,
    'Not to miss it,' you always say. 'Hold still'…
Corn, in its first green, pokes through old soil.

Lavender fields, grey and brown are tinged with mauve.
    The brinkmanship of spring – trading winter's gift of
                                  snow
for blowsy lanes where daisies grow and yellow grass

spills over. Apple blossom, cherry, cow parsley and
                                  elder,
    we watch it come, we see it go.

Isabel Bermudez

QUEENS MEADOW (SPRING EQUINOX)

A day stolen from the tide
Light rain, a haze of green ghosting the trees

Equal-handed the dark and the light
And I walk the middle way

Here where the blackbird sings rainsongs
And first bluebells push towards sky

Sway of curdwhite windflowers below the birches
Scudding of geese overhead

And this grace note: grazing the untended land between
watermeadow and road a trio of red deer

Roselle Angwin

Summer

A MOMENT OF MURMURATION

It took a cyclone of stubborn swallows to
fashion summer from a jumble of rain;

uncouple us from our resinous beds of
reed. Above the clouds we grew feathers

of wind; tumbling and soaring into each
other's drift like a storm of birdsong.

Chris Tutton

IN AUGUST

Light touches us. Dusk licks at bats.
And so I stand with aching feet
watching high beech leaves bunch,
then shift
in air too cool to lure our cats.
In lavender spikes, I hear first beat,
a thrumming moth. Ah now, they lift,
wingtips too fine for eyes to hold.
Stay. Stay. But those pulsed bodies pass,
like summer, slip, to whitening gold.

Alison Brackenbury

SHARING A RIDE

He seemed to love them more as his world shrank
from wheels to jumbled print.

They starred the small front garden every summer
noon-flowers unveiling otherworldly colours
pale yellow, orange-pink, all shades of mauve.

It's been ten years. I'm drawn to buy some seeds
Mixed sparkles? Harlequin? Maybe the mix whose name
conjures up thoughts of *The Arabian Nights?*

I make my choice - do what the packet says
and when midsummer dawns
a Magic Carpet's spread before my feet

each shut bloom coaxed by the June sun's bright wand
into a fabric from a fairy-tale.

I take a step.

Kathryn Daszkiewicz

TRIP SWITCH

It was the middle
of a month of summer storms.
Broad Beans mushed
and blackened in their pods
before they ripened.
Fat slugs the size of mice
gnawed the world back to the stalk,
glossed my night with patterns of slime,
and you turned up dripping at my door
wearing petrichor like cologne.

The house tried to warn me.
Something popped, sparked
and charred in the fuse box.
The lamp spat out the flimsy glass of its bulb
and you took over.
Light hummed on the tips of your teeth.
Moths flocked at the edges of your smile
and I too, wanted to tap your light.

When I awoke in the morning you'd gone.
Instead of a note, you'd left your outline
scorched into the bed sheets,
I imagined you leaving the house,
you – posting my hot key
back through the letter box,
you – sizzling as the morning mist
licked your skin.

76

I imagined you crackling
as you walked down my street
melting the hearts of women, stones,
dogs and men
burning yourself away from me.

Gaia Holmes

MORE WATER THAN LAND
after an untitled abstract painting by Katy Webster

She half-closes her eyes so
the world blurs against the window,
hills and fields transforming
to a view that seems more water than land.

The scene is so familiar she almost inhales
the sweet, damp smell of crops
soaking up the deluge; puddles mirroring
the fading sheen of an evening sky.

Daylight has already begun to ebb,
inviting night to creep in, and her own
reflection to supersede the countryside
of memories she journeys through.

She knows that not long after her face
becomes an apparition haunting the glass,
she'll arrive back in the place she grew up;
something tightens in her gut at the thought.

She closes her eyes fully,
blocks out the rain-smudged scenery,
feeling only the *thud-ah-thud, thud-ah-thud*
of the train rushing her home.

Judy Darley

FIRST DAY OF GLASTONBURY

This is the rain which licks the dust
from ivy, oxides, soot, grey grit
shaken from doormats, hot red dust
of Africa, particulates
from snowy lorries crammed with food.
The holly's thick skin celebrates.
Cities of leaf shake glistening hands.

This is the rain which turns the prize
white Persian to a grumpy sponge.

It is the rain on Europe's plain.
Danube and Elbe run brown with flood.
Villagers, firemen, pump in vain.
After two days, the hay crop fails.
The old Welsh mare, with heaving sides,
will cough till March, on mouldy bales.

Alison Brackenbury

THE LAST WOLF

'A carved stone by the side of the A9 near Brora claims to mark the site where the last wolf in Sutherland was killed by a man called Polson in 1700.'

And she won't write about snow, icicles on the inside of her windows, relief after all that hot, destructive rain. And she won't write about letting a lover go – that fucking American with his Harley and his Leica photographs, his Alaskan attitude to love. She won't write about the Istanbul bombings near the Blue Mosque, or the Paris explosions.

She'll write about George Mackay Brown, his awkward brilliance, integrity, his language full of fear of the female body, spilling over with the cadences of Orkney. She is brim-full of his Catholic taste, whisky. As she reads, she's beach-combing with George, whilst the sickle moon lies on its back. His Stromness summer was full of northern light that burnt his eyelids whilst he longed for sleep.

Right now, there's an indigo darkness in Alice's mind, a wind howling like the last living wolf and a call for the lifeboat out in the bay,

Anne Caldwell

80

WATCHING THE PERSEIDS WITH SUE

After our supper of cavolo nero,
black greens, from her brother's garden,
I dug in the woolly dark
of the cupboard under the stairs
for winter coats in August.
Outside the sky was clear
as just-cleaned windows,
every detail sharp, so
as we lay side by side
on my frayed alpaca blanket
looking up we felt flown
to another world, bathed
in radiance. When the rocks
and ice started falling, pencilling
the vast star-strewn ceiling
with their brief lines of light,
long vowels shot out of our mouths,
involuntarily ignited. We were kids
again, learning what beauty is –
there for a second, then gone –
giggling ourselves stupid. No idea
if it was awe or joy or the thrill
of self-forgetting, held safe there,
marinaded in dew, between earth,
heaven and the immensity
of all we'll never know.

Linda France

THE RESISTANCE OF MEMORY

We could live so well then,
in the cavernous emptiness of
each other's words; spend

idyllic holidays beached on
subterfuge, wade out of
our depth in clear blue water.

We could render the render of
our evenings nourishing then,
perch at the edge of the surf and

watch our reflections in the polished
half-full glass of things we hadn't said,
hardly finding words to notice

how the torch light dying lay
strewn around us like summers
buttoned up to the chin.

Chris Tutton

LARCOMBE LANE (SUMMER SOLSTICE)

Lanes on the cusp of honeysuckle and dog-rose
ash and oak in their full clothes.

Here where this damselfly alights
on the solar globe of the ox-eye daisy,
where the spells that make rain and wind
and tracks of birds pleach the air -

again and again we sing the sun back up,
spin summer-brief moonlight into our hair;
again and again in this circle of days and nights
against loss, death, decay we raise friendship, hope, love.

Brief lives; but what we're made of
is starstuff and water – everything holds our trace.

Roselle Angwin

BUILDING WITH SAND

In the beginning we didn't want sandcastles –
the sea was for swimming in, the sand
for barefoot running, or for lying on until
our hair and skin crackled dry with salt –

but when we saw those other families
building castles with crooked walls,
towers buckling under faded flags,
we decided we could do better

So, with bucket after bucket of damp sand
we constructed a castle: broad ramparts,
solid walls, sand packed hard as concrete –
not even a tsunami would knock it down.

Inside we made rooms, dragged in rocks
for tables and chairs, reeds to sleep on
and seaweed for curtains and blankets.
It was large enough for all of us

along with our yet-to-be-met husbands,
unborn children and grandchildren, friends,
relatives. We offered advice to our neighbours
as their castles fell each day to the tides.

The crabs surprised us – we didn't expect them
to scrape and burrow in the foundations, collapse
the walls, bury us in mountains of cold sand.
I dig all day, hope to find other survivors.

Kaye Lee

THE LONE TURNSTONE

left the quick pickings of flat rocks at low tide
his tortoiseshell summer colours
on the turn.

The sea wind over the Black Midden rocks
dispersed the warning of his skirling cry

as far as the velvet beds
and the site of the lost village near the bay

to cormorants on a stack
their blacks sun-greened

and Lizard Point where the defunct lighthouse stood
striped in Sunderland colours

past the grey stone wall
where the linnet
sang at dawn.

On reaching Potter's Hole

he made the break
(*interpres* – go between)

before the cold set in.

Kathryn Daszkiewicz

DIG

Holy Island, Northumberland, June 2017

Blackbird, tail up on the spoil-heap,
Eye pinned to the spade's bite –

Crumbs of soil
Clinging to his whiskers and his yellow trowel –
Flitting so lightly, no one has noticed him.

All week the shadows
Bend to the dull weight of flagstones,
An empty bucket, a wheelbarrow.

These hands – what have they done
But raise crude walls in the June drizzle,
Lose and uncover them again

In the time it takes a cock bird
To dart between the austere stone
War memorial and the black beacon.

Hands, minds, spade, chisel, hammer,
Bible and i-phone, grappling with Eternity. All week
They have heaped up rubble, and questions.

All their scribes, all their illuminations,
All the scholars of Europe and Palestine,
Seoul, Cupertino or England, cannot explain

This – in the quiet light
At dawn or the day's end, a blackbird
Opens his beak

And fourteen hundred summers are one summer.

Katrina Porteous

CRAB APPLE

That summer of 1976: thousands of ladybirds scrambling all over the privet, flitting from the honeysuckle to the crab apple tree, landing on our skin like spotted kisses. Concrete slabs beneath the washing line, hot as waffles. We squashed the ladybirds and red spider mites without mercy, our boredom treacle-thick punctuated by the rhythmic bounce of a tennis ball against a wall. There were endless evenings of roller skating up and down the same street. Standing next to a telephone box that smelt of rotten fruit trying to ring some boy without being overheard. Without our dad, our family house was eider-downed with grief.

Anne Caldwell

AN AGE OF REMEMBRANCE

In the monastery of your arms rests a
lawn of braille where I garden sleep,

by the millhouse of your summer lips
and the breath of your slumber song,

beneath the open parasol of your kiss,
among downy-soft hatchling mornings

where we seeded ourselves meadows of
wilder flowers; you, musk mallow pink,

shimmering down to the river
in a cloud of wings.

Chris Tutton

A LIFE

When I woke up, it had gone from winter to summer. I stepped outside into a meadow full of bright butterflies and hopping rabbits. I realised it was just a cartoon world, but I didn't know how to return to my own.

Over the hill was a pretty shepherd girl and an old man with a white beard. They nodded absurdly at me. I am not like you, I thought, I am real.

I came to the sea, but since it was a cartoon sea, would I get wet if I stepped into it? I was afraid to try, but here was a mermaid inviting me in. If I held her hand, would I feel it in mine? If she wanted to make love, what would I do?

Ian Seed

'HAVE SOME JAM -'
A LATE SUMMER PRESENT FROM AN
OLD FRIEND

Rich mould bloomed apple jelly.
Dark strawberries had turned tart.
I fear that the Tutti Frutti
was misconceived from the start.
With amber, crimson glugged away
I set one jar apart.
Let brief moon-daisies, blue cranesbill
preserve your August heart.

Alison Brackenbury

AUGUST FOR THE LOST BOYS

A hard time we had of it
In those endless days of summer.
Cricket? We were bad at it
And tennis was a bummer.

Swimming was too strenuous,
Golf far too expensive,
Sex might have made men of us
But the course was too intensive.

Guides were not our cup of tea,
Au pairs unobtainable,
And holidays beside the sea
Entirely unsustainable.

The English Riviera snored,
Blackpool was overrated.
The truth is we were mega-bored,
Scruffy and acne-plated.

A hard time we had of it,
No highlights to remember.
Autumn? We'd be glad of it.
Roll on September.

John Mole

BATS

Summer nights are like the Red Bull races;
stall turns, swoops, pulling Gs,
all by variable geometry of the wings,
not a supercharger or multi-bladed prop in sight.

Shadows flow and, even now, we want to be inside,
take the light of the day as memory.
Then the strange-faced ones
twitch and flicker awake, into flight.

Flying aces, their brain-screens
updated to the millisecond, take beetle, moth
in a million loss-of-separation incidents.
Fleets fly out of hanger-caves.

In this long Devon lane, a channel in a Death Star,
they rocket between hedges,
taking out rogue squadrons, lone invaders,
lightening the world's dark through force of life.

Simon Williams

SWALLOW SONG

Alone, I do not make a summer
    but, like a chandler, ply my ropes
        round the earth, woven from sand
           and rain, home and away.
      Call me a calligrapher of space,
    arcing the geometry of walls and doors,
the upturned cup of an arch;
    needle and compass, scratching sounds
        out of old-time discs, arrowing north
           and south and back again,
      hymn to beauty, ode to endurance.
I am aerial, attuned to invisible waves,
spiritual and brave, unburdened
    by distractions, what you say is sorrow,
        waste. I see what I see and I sing it.
           O Africa O peat brown river O feast
      of insects. Churning through sky soft as milk,
    my creamy breast's a lifted spoon,
and lifting, wings flung wide to the drift
    of air. Finding no edges, I raise the roof,
      a streak of wet slate, brushed ink ideogram
        of the child, still wise. If you only knew,
      today I open my auburn throat
    just for you – how much you can do
if you call a dream a dream
    and live it right through,
      untethered, year after year on the wing.

Linda France
95

THE CLOSING OF SUMMER

Through the roundel, the
wild goose steps out of

frame. Camera pans.
Anguish dresses the

stage in weeping ash.
Beneath a blind sun

The air is black with
the smoke of lovers.

Chris Tutton

Autumn

GOLDCRESTS

First sign, the faintest sound –
Invisible needlepoint tattoos the garden.
Whisked in on a south-east gale, fairy-lights

Twinkle in the apple-boughs,
Dapple and vanish, becoming leaves,
Becoming shadow. Where

Have they birled in from, this windfall
Bundle of contradictions, shy, hidden?
Black beetle eyes, thorn-stab, but round

And soft as plums, crowned brilliant
Ochre, as if each skull was split
Open, as earth is, by its own fire.

A flicker on the margin, their flight
And pin-prick calls' starlight glitters
Across day's drab garden, bringing

Wildness, and when they're gone –
Off in a whirl of blown leaves – the apple trees
Stand, for the first time, bare.

Katrina Porteous

AUTUMN EQUINOX

Sun shifts
in the trees,

bathes the table,
its slightly stale bread,

how sharp the world
is through the glass

as water slips
over the lip of the jug

at the equinox,
the half-way mark;

neither inclining to
nor away from the sun

but poised,
a round-bellied jug

where only a finger-mark
blurs the measure

of past and future.
Here at the tipping point,

the air's thick
with talk and birdsong

and the ghosts
are busy elsewhere

as time, our time,
pours from its vessel

a share of light equal
to the share of dark,

the quiet marriage
of glass and water

held to the
mirror
of the still, clear mind.

Isabel Bermudez

SEPTEMBER BUTTERFLY

I hadn't realized
a butterfly
could feast on blackberries,
could sink
proboscis through the
silk thin skin
and drink
juice, like a horse,
head lowered
at a stream.

As in a dream,
a dust of brown and amber spread
across the soft black cluster,
smudging close-clinging globes.

It cast a tint,
a hint of shades
the trees are only now
imagining,
as slightly tired leaves
plan their music
for their funeral.

A passing fly, a cloud
or wind catching the bush,
and this flash
of Autumn colours

shuts, like a door
bringing dusk.

For a moment it hangs,
quivering, grey-brown,
like last year's leaf
clinging fast to the last
to its source of life;
then shivers and rises effortlessly
to float high, bright
into the blue
sky.

Alwyn Marriage

STORIES

The ones she heard while she was drying her hair in front of the stove in the old farm kitchen. She never doubted that they were true. The chickens scratched around in the yard while she was scratching at the surface trying to understand the stories her mother harboured. She'd wake up in the night and rehearse one line she'd heard in the morning. She'd think about the day her grandfather died and she'd begged for more stories. She had her favourites of course. The one about the harvest moon and how it fades in the sky and the other that begins with a silence, a girl and then the cry of a bird. Now she craves more and more stories but they are all about words and seasons entwined with snow. She has no choice but to listen for its song.

Wendy French

NOVEMBER

(For Louis Milling, b. 24 November 2016)

November is reticent,
muffled in minor-key shades,
its shifting greys overlaid
with rusty gold and russet,
and faded flickering greens
turning marshy underfoot.

A November afternoon's
like the fifth act of a play
or final movement nearing
its recapitulation;
such suspended energy
withholding the dénouement.

But turn the corner and light
will splinter into your eyes,
as the lurking sun supplies
a scattered benediction.
November's enviable:
don't let them say otherwise.

Neil Powell

THE COLOURS MY MOTHER WORE

She wore the colours of these autumn trees
being, even in her heyday, autumnal.
She wove them into paintings, tapestries,
being, in art if not in discourse, subtle.

But when cataracts made them look too pale,
unknown to her, her flowers went fluorescent
and when miniatures hid behind a veil,
she painted sky on sky, letting the pigment,

the linseed oil, bloom of their own volition.
Skies hang in silver windows on my walls.
Live with a sunset, moon, a cloud formation –

they soon become part of the furniture.
And there's nothing under the sky but palls
if we can't see its subtlety or grandeur.

Mimi Khalvati

AUTUMN CROCUSES

'Shall I go through it all again?
The way my heart bursts through my chest,
and I'm on the cusp, between seasons?'
My time of year was always autumn, yours, too,
but back then we both agreed
we'd throw our lot in with the spring.

We walked in the gardens
and talked like this of seasons,
though really we were talking of other things.
'Who can argue with this blossom?' you said,
'It comes and comes, it doesn't fail...'
'I'd miss the seasons', 'I said, 'if I ever left again.'

Now here with you,
we circle a scattering of white and saffron
under the horse-chestnuts in the park.
Rain-swept, flayed, bruised as they are,
I pick them out as once you showed
me blossom; life's fragile candles,
her fodder for the dark.

Isabel Bermudez

HUKENTOR, NEAR MERRIVALE
(AUTUMN EQUINOX)

Where dawn spreads out across the moor
wild like a storm of horses
where the rowan berries are backlit
a shower of rubies stalled in flight
where I'm cupped in the land's ancient palm

where he comes down off these hills
like an oak-king, bringing all of himself
to the feast, singing the land back into herself
for the winter's dreaming, bringing the songs
that will make a harvest of these days –

words writing themselves in rock, tree, water.

Roselle Angwin

CAFÉ AMSTERDAM
(after a photo by Marco Savic, National Geographic)

Jurgen felt I should have gone outside with the cigar,
although the law has yet to reach this small corner of the
                                                    old city.

I told him I've been smoking here for years, the
                                bartender doesn't mind
and since there's just Jurgen, him and me, he gets the
                                        casting vote

So we talk over the day's excreta, as the light grows
                                            shorter;
evening comes through old Maam Ackerman's
                                apartments opposite.

Two more Duvals are the last glimpses of the sun
before the tired lamps become the way we see each
                                        other's faces.

The café fills. Jurgen leaves to join his family. Alene and
                                Lina's posters
smile down over the Americanos. I take my next cigar
                        onto Rozamunda Straat.

Simon Williams

THIRD QUARTER

That this happened then that it will not
happen again that you misremember
that you thought this was an evening
some weeks after you had first slept together
yet the page proves you wrong
it was just a passionate few days before
and that she must have guessed
how you were going to respond
that it was she who made the bold suggestion
knowing you were gauche and naïve
too slow in coming forward
and how tenderly she must have smiled
to think you thought you had read the signs
when really they sped over your head
as migrating birds have done
in all these intervening years
taking with them the summer's warmth

before the chill and now these pages read
so much like fiction
the excited narrator proving unreliable
too wrapped up in himself
in what looks satirical yet now reading it back
it makes you step out taller even so –
why should it make your hands and shoulders
vibrate with nothing more
than just moving here in disconnected time
in this quite other place

is it a reminder that you were once loved
that you loved her as much
that you managed to catch it well enough
with some turn of phrase
or is it no more than a clear affirmation
you trod the earth in some distant year
defiant in the way you walk here

except that now (as you did not then) you understand
her imperative to wake keenly as you can
to every moment remembering how you walked
down an incline hand in hand that September
to one side the impersonal plate-glass window
of a gymnasium defended on your left
by diamond shapes of a tall wire fence
that you stood there in the blue autumn evening
not knowing for sure
that rain would fall in a matter of minutes
that you'd be lovers before the week was out
that there'd be tears and no reconciliation
that you'd both go your separate ways
long before the New Year's buds had broken

Martyn Crucefix

NOVEMBER

I was sitting on a park bench, thinking of an old friend, of how I had never embraced him. I hadn't seen him for years, and yet as I was wondering about him, I saw him pass by in the light rain that had started to fall. He turned and stared as if he could not believe it was really me. He seemed to have hardly changed, while I had aged almost beyond recognition. I got up and ran to take him in my arms, to hold him so close I could stop his eyes from wandering over my face.

Ian Seed

THE MOTH ROOM

He follows her home from the ball, trailing in the pitch of her laughter: bright as glass, bleak as snow. She's taken off her shoes for dancing, runs barefoot through the ragged streets, giggles falling from her lips and glinting in her wake.

The warehouse she leads him to is shuttered into rooms, each with its own door to unlock. Hers is labelled The Moth Room, and when he asks why, she stands on tiptoe to reach a high shelf, draws down a narrow box. "They're in here," she breathes. "Unless these are the wasp carapaces I collect." She fires a glance at him, and he flinches as he spies the sting in her eyes. "No, I'm sure of it, this is the moths."

At her bidding, he peels off the lid, reveals layer upon layer of little furry stiffs – some brittle and brown as rolled-up autumn leaves, others banded with scarlet and gold.

"Where are their wings?" he gasps.

And laughing, she spins, showing off the rustle and flutter of her nip-waisted gown, all the layers ashimmer in the glow of October's moon.

Judy Darley

STORIES

Distress

a leaf is hopping
it lifts   its frail head
knocks at a stone
shakes slightly   judders
and sways   falls back
tries to raise itself
its single leaf-wing
still breathes
dry   hop-hopping
sipping at gravel

No loading

a flock of them   skitters   whirls up
maddened   desperate to keep together
a few not swept up   striving   to join the others
almost catching up   tossed aside   mid-flight
as the great crowd   crosses   the double yellow lines
lands on   NO LOADING   then nearly all of them
swept away   to spin just above   the concourse
and arrive again on   NO LOADING

With abandon

Bowling along   spiralling   it suddenly
flutters down   lands flat on its leaf-back
and encircling it   at different heights
the tall grasses are perpetually
sumptuously   agitated

Moniza Alvi

AUTUMN

A scent of earth as it slowly exhales,
things bed down, are buried
then churned; worms and beetles,
old matter, dead leaves; rain
feeding late sun as the colours drain;
red of the gold-finches,
the sparrows' dun,
and those three visiting sisters,
the fates. *Homesick, Heartache and Rue*
who thread the season's changes;
light the sky with a pale full moon,
drape cold air in mist and wood-smoke
and draw our tales from the dark, moist earth
as the gaping dawn is filled with blue.

Isabel Bermudez

AT STOVER PARK

1

What is in the dark jade lake,
constantly changing; this element
trees live by, lean into and draw from?
Is water calling time to let go?
Small fish arrow in liveries
of gold, brown and spangled green.

Autumn is the colours they are,
as they shift in a mirror of branches
to follow the leader, surfacing softly.
Smoke from a logging fire penetrates
everything, gutsy and pungent,
as woodland tends to its wounds.

2

This is the time of symmetry,
equinoctial – a word-sound, technical
as a wheel; its spokes in the earth.

Here is the place of twins,
soft grey shades in the sky
are the colours of a tern's wing.

Water is forging doubles,
each bird is being two – one is feathered
and, upside down, one is water.

Leaves in millions fold over
and drop into some dark voice
behind the light.

3

Swans are mute.
Swans are perfection.

Nothing will tame them
into a poem.

4

Everything green
still, on resonant water;
suddenly dragonflies.

Susan Taylor

THE LONELINESS OF LOMBARDY POPLARS

Giant quills by which the wind-shy
try to rewrite storm-harried fenland:

a line of trees where no trees grow.
In winter, stark lines of charcoal

against the snow, holding back
nothing. In June they are green

cheerleaders shaking plumes
with up-stretched arms, holding back

nothing while nonchalant clouds
roll on. They shed gold leaves

in an October striptease, holding
back nothing, holding onto

nothing. A gull drifts by
the ruin of a windmill.

The sea is far from here.

Kathryn Daszkiewicz

ALONG THE ROAD

In Sussex, late
from the last bus
driving deep woods at night
I see the stag
trot headlamps' beam

rut in his blood
antlered by light.

Alison Brackenbury

SAMUEL PALMER'S *YELLOW TWILIGHT*

The time of between
has been consumed:
it is no longer
an interim measure,
or the glow
of serene fading

But rages everywhere,
a choking climate
that could have started
as a single spark
or God
investing one bush

But now, set
beyond remorse,
beyond the reach
of any helicoptered
douche
it is past quenching

It has become
prescient, to be read
while there is time
before the paper
itself
catches fire

Lawrence Sail

THE FALLOW YIELD

The old man hummed quietly in the cool shade beside a watchtower of sorrow, winding the last burnished yarn of summer onto a skein. In the crowing breeze, tambourine leaves turned slowly to autumn, and sated geese flew swollen into a prodigal spread. The old man paused for a moment, rested his song, and briefly read the gnarled journal of his worn hands as a stranger. 'Soon the river will flow too fast, and become too cold to bathe in,' thought the old man, as he felt the soft twine slip through his fingers, 'and I will taste nothing but the flavour of winter.' In the mewing distance, a crimson veined evening purred, and bedded unfurled claws into the fraying skyline.

As the old man continued to reflect on the passing season, a white mule laden with apples appeared at his side.

The white mule affably extended a cordial salutation, which the old man, although unable to remember any previous encounter with the mule, returned with the warm, easy grace of a fond acquaintance. 'I have often glimpsed you from afar, standing atop the tower, old man,' the mule began, 'and each time have I attempted to understand the purpose of your surveillance.'

The old man would have preferred to remain alone and continue to fix the thread of his broken melody, but he felt awkwardly answerable to the mule's amiable gaze and accordingly scratched his grey bearded chin pensively, allowing himself a few uncomfortable seconds to form his reply.

'Every day, I have climbed this lofty tower and watched. But I am a foolish old man and my vision is dimming. Each sunrise I see less than I did the sunset before, and I watch little but the day receding from my grasp,' he lamented, at once feeling ashamed of his complaint.

'What do you wish to see, old man?' the white mule posed, with a sympathetic smile.

'The expected. Or the unexpected. It makes no difference,' sighed the old man. 'What I wish to see I shall not, and I must settle for any view in its absence.'

Crickets clicked chattering heels, and a peel of cattle bells clanged a languid chorus to accompany the late afternoon's slovenly passage.

'Once, I looked out onto a colourful distance which seemed to stretch endlessly into the blue sky, and everywhere I looked, I saw myself threshing grain, herding sheep, fishing clear streams. But, now I look upon a distance which has caught up with me and I am unable to find myself there.'

'You hoard your sadness as a sleepless old man gathers over-ripe fruit from the tree of dreams, with no thought for the usefulness of his harvest,' the mule advised, shaking its head softly to and fro.

The old man fell silent for a moment and thought hard on the white mule's words.

'My harvest feeds me well enough. I am an old man and I need nothing more than I can take without reaching.'

'You eat the fruit within your reach, yet the fruit is bitter

123

and you complain of its flavour. How does this satisfy you?'

'I am satisfied by the memory of how it once tasted, even though it has become unpalatable to me now.'

'You have grown fat on your sorrow, old man, perhaps you would care to walk with me for a while, and I will show you a sweeter fruit, ripe for the picking.'

The old man thanked the mule gratefully, but made no attempt to stand. 'Perhaps I will find a sweeter fruit of my own soon,' he mused, as he watched the mule retreat. 'Farewell then, old man,' bid the white mule, turning and beginning to walk slowly away. 'I have a long journey ahead, and I must not delay. But I shall remember you well, and I shall think of you often. And I shall see you always in an endless distance, regardless of my station, or whatever view lies before me.'

Chris Tutton

WHEEL

The winds travelling
in their great pereginations –
the migrations of spring,
updraught of summer,
autumn calling it all back,
winter's frosty unbirthings.

How is it we ever fear we're lost,
caught up in this perennial trawlnet
slipstreaming the seasons
through a million trillion galaxies? –
This finding, this holding,
This once-and-for-all belonging.

Roselle Angwin

ACKNOWLEDGEMENTS

'Stories' by Moniza Alvi from 'Blackbird, Bye Bye' Bloodaxe Books (2018) Reproduced with permission of Bloodaxe Books. 'Cow Parsley', 'Autumn Crocuses' and 'Autumn' by Isabel Bermudez from "Small Disturbances" Rockingham Press 2016. 'Spring' and 'Autumn Equinox' by Isabel Bermudez from "Sanctuary" Rockingham Press 2018 'The Green Plover' and 'March 4th' by Alison Brackenbury first published in "Stand Magazine', 'Have Some Jam; A Late Present From an Old Friend' by Alison Brackenbury published in "Poetry Spotlight" 'In August' by Alison Brackenbury published in "Domestic Cherry" 'First Day of Glastonbury' by Alison Brackenbury published in "The North" 'Mothering Sunday' by Alison Brackenbury published in "The Reader", 'Spring Comes When' by Alison Brackenbury published in "Beyond Spring" by Matthew Oates. Fair Acre Press 2017, and in "Artemis Poetry" 'Along the Road' by Alison Brackenbury first published in "Rialto".
'Pruning the Magnolia' by John Daniel from "Skinning the Bull". Oversteps Books.
'Wild Garlic' by Mark Gwynne-Jones from "In the Light of This" Route.
'Questions' by Mimi Khalvati first appeared in"The Compass" 'Villa Joyosa' by Mimi Khalvati first appeared in "A Restricted View fom under the hedge" 'Street' by Mimi Khalvati first appeared in "Agenda".
'Spring Camping' by Alwyn Marriage, first published in "Notes from a Camper Van", Bellhouse Books 2014. 'September Butterfly' by Alwyn Marriage from "Touching Earth" Oversteps Books 2007 and "Shropshire Butterflies" Fair Acre Press 2011.
'Foula, Auld Yule' by Katrina Porteous, previously published in "100 Island Poems of Great Britain and Ireland" edited by James Knox Whiltet. Iron Press 2005. 'Dig' by Katrina Porteous previously published in "Many Hands", Peregrini Lindisfarne Landscape Partnership 2017. 'November' by Neil Powell first published in "Acumen".

'Insect' by Ian Seed from "Shifting Registers" Shearman Press, 'A Life' by Ian Seed from "Makers of Empty Dreams" Shearsman Press and 'November' by Ian Seed from "Identity Papers" Shearsman Press. "Winter Loving' by Anne Stewart first appeared in "The Frogmore Papers" Issue 70, 2007 and in "The Janus Hour" 2014, Oversteps Books.

'Seasons of Winter' and ' The Fallow Yield' by Chris Tutton from "Seasons of Winter" (Avalanche Books 2005) 'A Moment of Murmuration', 'An Age of Remembrance' and 'The Resistance of Memory' by Chris Tutton from "Impossible Memories" (Avalanche Books 2016) 'The Closing of Summer' by Chris Tutton from "Angles of Repose" (Avalanche Books 2012)